BUDDIES

by Peter J. Downing   illustrated by Loreen Leedy

HARCOURT BRACE & COMPANY

Orlando Atlanta Austin Boston San Francisco Chicago Dallas New York
Toronto London

Ben and Marty were always friends.
They were buddies—through thick
and thin.
When Ben got scratched by a cat,
Marty was there to help.

Boo Boo Aides

3

When Marty lost his backpack, Ben found it.
They were always buddies—through thick and thin.

Then Andy moved into the
neighborhood.
Things began to change.
When Marty called Ben, Ben was
playing with "the new boy."

When Marty saw Ben at school,
Andy was with him.
When Marty needed help, Ben and
Andy were too busy.

Things were different.
It looked like Andy was Ben's new buddy.
No more "thick and thin."

"Hey, Marty! Want to play pogs?"
asked Ben.
"With you?" asked Marty.
"With Andy and me," Ben said.
Marty thought about friends through
thick and thin.
"No," said Marty.

"Ben told me that you're a great player," said Andy.
"He did?" asked Marty.
"Sure. He talks about you all the time," said Andy.
"He does?" asked Marty.

"You're my buddy, aren't you?" said Ben.
"Will you be my buddy, too?" asked Andy.
"Yeah," said Marty. "Through thick and thin."